Ready for lift-off?
Log your name here:

....

To my very special friends,
Nick White and Laura Beckett.

— BN

This is a second edition, first published in 2018 by Flying Eye Books,
an imprint of Nobrow Ltd. 27 Westgate Street, London E8 3RL.

Illustrations by Ben Newman. Text by Dominic Walliman and Avalon Nuovo.

3 5 7 9 10 8 6 4 2

Published in the US by Nobrow (US) Inc.

Printed in Latvia on FSC® certified paper.

ISBN: 978-1-911171-55-3

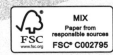

www.flyingeyebooks.com

PROFESSOR ASTRO CAT'S
SPACE ROCKETS

DR DOMINIC WALLIMAN & BEN NEWMAN

•FLYING EYE BOOKS•
LONDON | NEW YORK

TRAVELLING THROUGH SPACE

When you look up at the sky at night, you are actually looking into outer space. How cool is that?

All of those tiny lights are stars and planets that are millions of miles away. If we got closer, we would see that they are actually very big. Many are even bigger than planet Earth.

PROFESSOR ASTRO CAT

FELICITY

In order to learn about space, we send **astronauts** or **space probes** to these places. Would you like to see? Let's go!

ASTRO MOUSE

HOW DO YOU GET TO SPACE?

First we need to leave Earth. We can't just jump into the air and float into space, because gravity is very strong.

Gravity is the force that pulls everything towards the Earth. When you jump up and then fall back down, this is gravity at work!

We need to use a special vehicle with a huge amount of energy to beat the powerful pull of gravity. This vehicle is called a rocket.

ROCKETS

A rocket's engine is like a car's, except that it burns a lot more fuel and it is much hotter!

When the rocket fuel burns, it pushes out hot gas. The gas moves so fast towards the ground that it pushes the rocket upwards.

A similar thing happens if you let go of a balloon that has air inside. The air rushes out of it, making it fly around!

HISTORY OF SPACE TRAVEL

In 1947, the first living beings were sent into space. It wasn't safe for people yet, so instead they sent fruit flies.

After that, scientists began to send other animals into space. Some of the first were a dog called Laika and a monkey called Albert.

In 1961, a Russian man named Yuri Gagarin became the first person to travel in space. He went around the Earth once on a rocket.

APOLLO 11

Here is the Apollo 11 capsule. In the year 1969, it carried the first humans to ever walk on the moon.

Apollo 11 was enormous, but the astronauts only had this small area to live in during the eight-day mission.

STAGE 3 ROCKET

STAGE 2 ROCKET

STAGE 1 ROCKET

USA

USA

USA

The rest of Apollo 11 contained rockets. It took three stacked on top of each other to launch Apollo 11 into space.

STAGES OF THE LAUNCH

This is the stage 1 rocket. It got
Apollo 11 off the ground and into space.
Once it had no fuel left, it broke away.

Then, the stage 2 rocket **ignited**
and pushed further into space.
After that, it broke away too.

The stage 3 rocket got Apollo 11 close to the moon and then it fell away, releasing the Lunar Module and the Command/Service Module.

Then the Lunar Module separated from the Command/Service Module and headed for the moon.

LANDING ON THE MOON

The Lunar Module was a small vehicle that could separate itself from the spacecraft. The astronauts on Apollo 11 used it to successfully land on the moon.

Two astronauts landed on the moon,
while the third stayed in the spacecraft. They collected
rocks to bring back for scientists to study.

When they were done, the Lunar Module's small rocket engines launched them back into space to rejoin the Command/Service Module.

GETTING BACK TO EARTH

LUNAR MODULE

APOLLO 11

Once all three astronauts were back on Apollo 11, the Lunar Module was left to float away.

Finally, the Service Module broke off and floated away, as it was no longer needed.

All that was left was this small part, the Command Module.

The Command Module fell back to Earth very fast, and got very hot! When it was close enough to Earth, it used a parachute to land safely in the ocean.

MODERN SPACE SHUTTLES

Around 10 years after Apollo 11, scientists created a new kind of spacecraft: a space shuttle.

The space shuttle had a massive rocket to get it into space. After it launched, the rocket fell away, and the shuttle could fly with its own engine.

Space shuttles could orbit around Earth and then land just like aeroplanes. One space shuttle could be used many times, as long as it had a new rocket for every launch!

GREAT SHUTTLES AND THEIR MISSIONS

This is Columbia. It was the first space shuttle to go into space and land back on Earth. It ran 27 successful missions!

Here is Discovery. It carried the Hubble Space Telescope, which lets us take pictures of very distant stars and planets!

Challenger had nine successful missions. It carried the first American woman, Sally Ride, and the first African American person, Guion Bluford, into space!

OUR NEXT MISSION: TO MARS AND BEYOND

We don't use space shuttles anymore. Scientists are working on a new spacecraft called Orion.

Orion will use newer, better rockets called the Space Launch System. They will be the most powerful rockets ever built!

Orion will be able to carry astronauts to Mars and beyond. This is much further than any spacecraft has ever gone!

ROCKETS FOR ALL!

Soon, ordinary people may be able to travel on rockets! Many people are designing rockets for space tourism. Imagine having your summer holiday on the moon or even on Mars!

In the far future, we may be able to use rockets to travel to other stars in the galaxy and even settle on other Earth-like planets! Stay tuned, space explorers. Maybe you will have your own rocket someday! Until then, keep looking towards the stars.

GLOSSARY

Astronaut A person who has been trained to travel in space.

Space Probe A spacecraft for exploring space and other planets. It is controlled by computers back on Earth.

Orbit The oval-shaped movement of a planet or moon around a star or another planet.

Spacecraft A vehicle that can travel in space.

Ignite To make something burn or heat up strongly.